Pens Activity Bible

CWR

Introducing Pens

Charlotte Chalk
Cheerful and chirpy, she loves to sing! She's always happy to join in the fun whatever the day brings.

Sharpy
He's lively, he's loveable, he knows how to get himself in a mess – and he's Pens' very best friend.

Denzil the Pencil
He's definitely the King of Cool, although perhaps not always as confident as he likes to make out.

Gloria Glitter-pen
She's fabulously fashionable and adores hats. A bit of a fusspot maybe, but still there for a friend in need.

Marco Marker
He's a joker who loves messing about, but he always means well, even if he sometimes gets things wrong.

Philippa Feltpen
A real peacemaker, she helps keep the other Pens in order by sorting out arguments and giving good advice.

Waxy Max
He's very sporty and football mad. On the outside, he's tough, but underneath he's got the biggest heart.

Squiggle and Splodge
The Scribble twins! They're both quiet, both shy. Although they may not look alike, they do almost everything together.

Copyright © CWR 2014

Published 2014 by CWR, Waverley Abbey House, Waverley Lane, Farnham, Surrey GU9 8EP, UK. CWR is a Registered Charity – Number 294387 and a Limited Company registered in England – Registration Number 1990308.

The right of Alexa Tewkesbury to be identified as the author of this work has been asserted by her in accordance with the Copyright, Designs and Patents Act 1988; sections 77 and 78.

All rights reserved. No part of this publication may be reproduced, stored in a retrieval system, or transmitted, in any form or by any means, electronic, mechanical, photocopying, recording or otherwise, without the prior permission in writing of CWR.

For list of National Distributors visit www.cwr.org.uk/distributors

Concept development, editing, design and production by CWR
Illustrations by Mike Henson

Printed in Croatia by Zrinski

ISBN: 978-1-78259-153-5

Presented to:

_____

From:

_____

Date:

_____

Contents

Old Testament

The Very Beginning	10
In God's Garden	16
When the Rain Came Down	22
God's Good Friends	28
The Wrong Son	34
Moses, God's Hero	40
Spies in Canaan	46
Gideon, the Brave and Mighty	52
A Baby for Hannah	58
A New King	64
Solomon, the Wise	70
Nehemiah Builds a New City	76
The Man God Chose	82

New Testament Contents

The Baby in the Stable	90
The Boy Who Wasn't Lost	96
The First Followers	102
Just Like Mary	108
God's Love	114
The Seed Story	120
The One Who Came Back	126
The Water-Walker	132
Alive and Well!	138
The Fantastic Party	144
Jesus in Jerusalem	150
God's Great Plan	156
Out of the Tomb!	162
Jesus' Promise	168
Answers	174

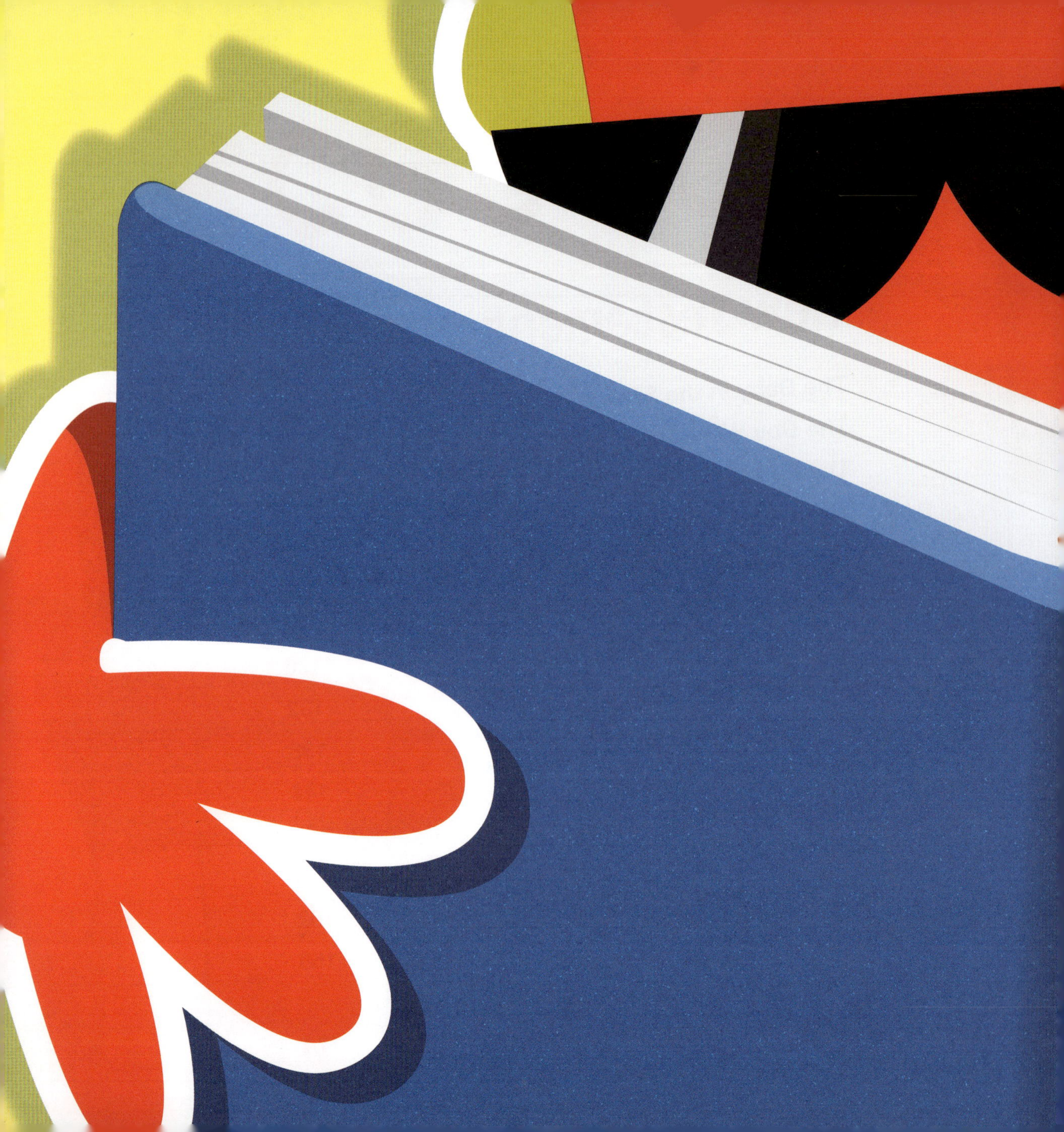

The Old Testament

The Very Beginning
Genesis 1 and 2

When God began to make the universe, there were just stormy seas and darkness.

'I'm going to make something beautiful here,' He smiled. 'Let's have some light.'

At once, the darkness was gone and there was brilliant light everywhere!

'That's good,' God nodded.

It was the very first day.

On the second day, God said, 'What we need is ... SKY!'

And there it was! A blue-bright sky above the stormy seas.

'Perfect,' God nodded happily. 'Now, my world needs some good, firm ground.'

So on the third day, the seas rolled back and the dry land appeared.

'I'd like things to grow here,' God said.

And they did! Grass and trees, flowers and fruit.

The Very Beginning

The fourth day came.

God said, 'Let's put some lights in the sky.
A sun for the daytime.
A moon for the night.'

God scattered stars, too, in huge handfuls.

On the fifth day, He said, 'Let's fill the waters with life!'

Suddenly, oceans and rivers splish-splashed with fish of every colour and creatures of every size.

Next, God commanded, 'Sky! Be full of things that fly!'

Out they came – birds and insects and flitting bats.

On the sixth day, God cried, 'Animals next!'

And wildlife appeared – creeping, running, leaping.

'Now,' said God excitedly, 'the most special part of all: people, to enjoy my world and take care of it.'

God welcomed His new friends. Then He looked around Him.

'Good,' He said. 'And, tomorrow, I think I'll have a rest.'

The Very Beginning

Look at the ocean in the picture. How many sea creatures can you see?

Now count the arms and legs on the crab. How many are there?

Colour in God's beautiful world!

In God's Garden
Genesis 2 and 3

God made a perfect world. He made a man and a woman to live there, too. The man was called Adam and the woman, Eve. God gave them a beautiful garden where fruit grew on the trees.

'Help yourselves,' God smiled. 'But don't touch the tree in the middle. Its fruit is bad for you. If you eat it, you won't be able to stay here with me.'

A snake lived in God's garden.

The snake didn't care about God. It just wanted to make trouble.

The snake asked Eve, 'Did God tell you not to eat the fruit from that tree in the middle?'

'Yes,' Eve replied. 'If we do, it will make God sad. We won't be able to stay with Him.'

In God's Garden

'Nonsense!' laughed the snake. 'If you eat that fruit, you'll know everything God knows. And God doesn't want you to.'

'I'd *like* to know everything God knows!' Eve thought. 'Perhaps I'll eat just a little bit.'

So Eve picked some fruit and ate it. She gave some to Adam, too.

But it made them sad. Suddenly, they knew how it felt to do something wrong – and it felt bad.

'Why did you eat the fruit I told you not to?' God asked. 'Here in the garden you had everything you needed. Why wasn't it enough?'

He added sadly, 'I'll always love you, but you can't stay here. I gave you so much. Now you will have to leave with nothing.'

Adam and Eve's friendship with God was broken.

But He had a plan to put things right again …

In God's Garden

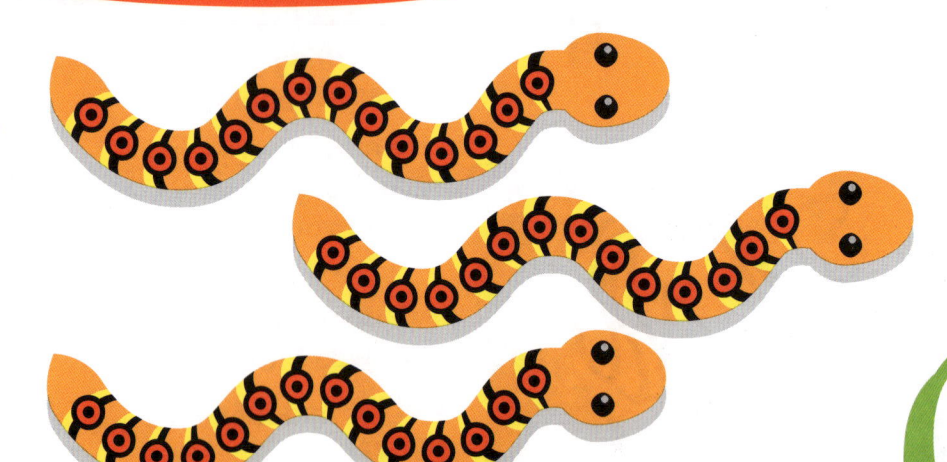

Which snake is the odd one out? Draw a circle around it.

Now draw a long, wiggly tongue coming out of each snake's mouth.

What kind of fruit is in Charlotte's hand?
Join the dots to find out.

21

When the Rain Came Down
Genesis 6, 7 and 8

God had created a beautiful world. But the people who lived there were spoiling it. They thought bad thoughts and did bad things.

So God decided to make the world new again. He'd send rain to wash it clean.

One man called Noah was kind and good. God wanted to keep him safe.

God said to Noah, 'Build a boat for you, your family, and two of each kind of animal.'

So Noah set to work.

When the boat was finished, Noah, his family and all the animals clambered aboard. Then God closed the door behind them.

That's when the rain started.

It poured down in HUGE drops. Day after day. Night after night.

The land disappeared under all the water!

But Noah trusted God.

'When He is ready,' Noah thought, 'the sun will come out again.'

When the Rain Came Down

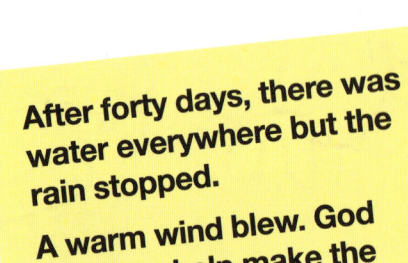

After forty days, there was water everywhere but the rain stopped.

A warm wind blew. God sent it to help make the floods go down.

Noah said to a little dove, 'Go outside. See if there is any dry land yet.'

Off she flew. And when she didn't come back to the boat, Noah smiled.

'She must have found somewhere dry to live,' he thought.

Noah, his family and all the animals stepped out of the boat.

'My world is brand-new,' God said. 'Now you must all fill it with your children, so that there will be plenty of people and animals to live here again.'

Then God put a rainbow across the sky as a promise – He would never send so much rain ever again.

'Thank You,' smiled Noah.

When the Rain Came Down

Can you show Noah's ark the way to dry land?

Noah took two of every kind of animal on the ark with him and his family. Join the dots to find out what animal Denzil is riding on.

27

God's Good Friends
Genesis 17, 18 and 21

Abraham was God's friend. He knew that God loved him and wanted the best for him. So whenever God spoke to him, he always listened.

One day, God said, 'Abraham! I want you and your wife, Sarah, to move house. I'm going to show you somewhere much better to live. Somewhere to have a family.'

So Abraham and Sarah packed everything up and set off on their journey.

Abraham and Sarah liked their new home. But they were sad. God had made them a promise.

'Your family will grow and grow!' He had said. 'One day there will be as many of them as there are stars in the sky!'

But Abraham and Sarah had no children at all. And they were old now – much too old to have a baby.

God's Good Friends

Abraham did trust God, but this promise was just a little too hard to believe.

So when God said, 'I'm going to give you a son,' Abraham couldn't help laughing.

'Can a man as old as I am really have a baby?' he chuckled to himself.

Sarah laughed, too.

'At my age?' she giggled. 'I don't think so!'

But God knew what He was going to do.

A little while later, Abraham and Sarah's baby son was born.

They smiled down at their little boy.

'I shall call you Isaac,' Abraham said.

God smiled, too.

He'd given Abraham and Sarah a wonderful present.

And from Isaac would grow a huge family of grandchildren and great-grandchildren – just as God had promised.

God's Good Friends

Abraham and Sarah had lots to pack up when they moved to their new home. When Gloria goes on holiday, she takes a lot of things, too.

How many suitcases does she have?

Draw a circle around the biggest suitcase and a square around the smallest.

God gave His friends, Abraham and Sarah, an amazing present! Here's another present. Colour it in to make it look really exciting!

The Wrong Son
Genesis 25 and 27

Isaac and Rebecca were married, and had two sons. They were twins. Esau was born first. His skin was very hairy. Just afterwards, came Jacob.

The two boys were quite different.

Esau loved to be outside and was good at hunting.

Jacob was quiet and liked to stay at home.

Esau was Isaac's favourite son.

Jacob was Rebecca's.

One day, when Isaac was old and blind, he said to Esau, 'Go out hunting. Catch something I like. Then when you get back, cook me a meal. After I've eaten it, I shall give you my special blessing.'

Rebecca heard what Isaac said.

But she didn't want Esau to have Isaac's blessing. She wanted Isaac to bless Jacob.

The Wrong Son

'Jacob!' Rebecca whispered. 'Your father is going to give Esau his special blessing. Do as I say, and you shall have it instead!'

Rebecca cooked a meal for Isaac. She told Jacob to dress up in Esau's clothes. Then she covered his arms in goatskin. Isaac couldn't see Jacob because he was blind. But if he touched him, now Jacob's skin would feel hairy like Esau's.

Jacob took his father the meal Rebecca had cooked.

'Here you are, Father,' he said.

'That's Jacob's voice,' Isaac replied. He touched the goatskins on Jacob's arms. 'But you feel like Esau.'

So Isaac ate his meal. Then he asked God to bless his son, and he made him head of the family.

But it was the wrong son!

When Esau found out what Jacob had done, he was very angry.

And Isaac was very sad.

The Wrong Son

These pictures of Jacob dressed in Esau's clothes all look the same. But one is different.

Put a tick beside the odd one out.

Max and Sharpy are going to a super-hero party. What could they dress up in to make them look like super-heroes? Draw in their costumes and colour them.

39

Moses, God's Hero
Exodus 3 and 4

Moses was a shepherd.

'I'm a very ordinary man,' he thought. 'I do very ordinary things.'

One day he was looking after his sheep and goats when suddenly –

'That bush is on fire!' he cried.

But the fire wasn't burning the bush. It just flickered and danced among the leaves.

Then came a voice from deep inside the flames: 'Moses! Moses!'

Moses took a step closer.

'Stay there!' the voice commanded. 'Take off your shoes. I am the Lord your God. The ground you are standing on is holy.'

Moses couldn't believe his ears!

'The king of Egypt is being very unkind to my people, the Israelites,' God said. 'I've chosen YOU, Moses, to set them free.'

'But I'm nobody,' Moses mumbled. 'Who's going to take any notice of *me*?'

Moses, God's Hero

God answered, 'I will be with you. Tell my people that I have sent you.'

'But supposing they don't believe me?' Moses frowned.

God said, 'Throw the stick you're holding onto the ground.'

Moses did. Instantly, the stick turned into a snake!

'Aah!' yelled Moses.

God said, 'Now pick the snake up.'

'What?!' Moses gasped.

But, carefully, he took hold of the snake – and it became a stick again!

'Show this to my people,' God commanded. 'Then they'll have to believe I sent you.'

'But how can *I* go to Egypt?' Moses muttered. 'I won't know what to say to people.'

'Trust me,' God replied. 'I will give you the right words. Take your brother, Aaron, with you. He's good at talking. Now, off you go.'

So ordinary Moses went off to do something EXTRAordinary for God.

Moses, God's Hero

How many sheep does Moses have?

And how many goats?

How many animals does Moses have altogether?

Look carefully at these five burning bushes. Only two of them are exactly the same. Which two is it? Draw a line to join them.

Spies in Canaan
Joshua 2

After Moses, God chose Joshua to be the new leader of His special people.

God said to Joshua, 'I'm giving my people somewhere new to live: the land of Canaan. And I want YOU to lead them there. But don't worry, Joshua,' God smiled, 'I will always be with you.'

Joshua sent two spies into Canaan.

'See what you can find out,' he ordered. 'But don't get caught!'

When the two spies reached the city of Jericho, they stayed in the house of a woman called Rahab.

But it wasn't long before the king of Jericho heard about them.

Bang, bang, BANG!

The king's men thumped on Rahab's door.

'Where are the spies?' they shouted.

Quickly, Rahab hid Joshua's men up on the roof. Then she opened the door.

Spies in Canaan

'Some men *were* here,' she smiled. 'But they left through the city gate. Hurry and you'll catch them.'

Off went the king's men, while Rahab ran back to the spies.

'I know that God has given you this land,' she said. 'That's why I've saved you. Please be kind to my family and to me.'

The spies gave Rahab a piece of red rope.

'Fetch your family into your house,' they said. 'Then tie this rope to your window. When we march into Jericho, we will all see the rope and you will be safe.'

Back with Joshua, the spies said, 'We're ready to move into the land of Canaan. God really has given it to us.'

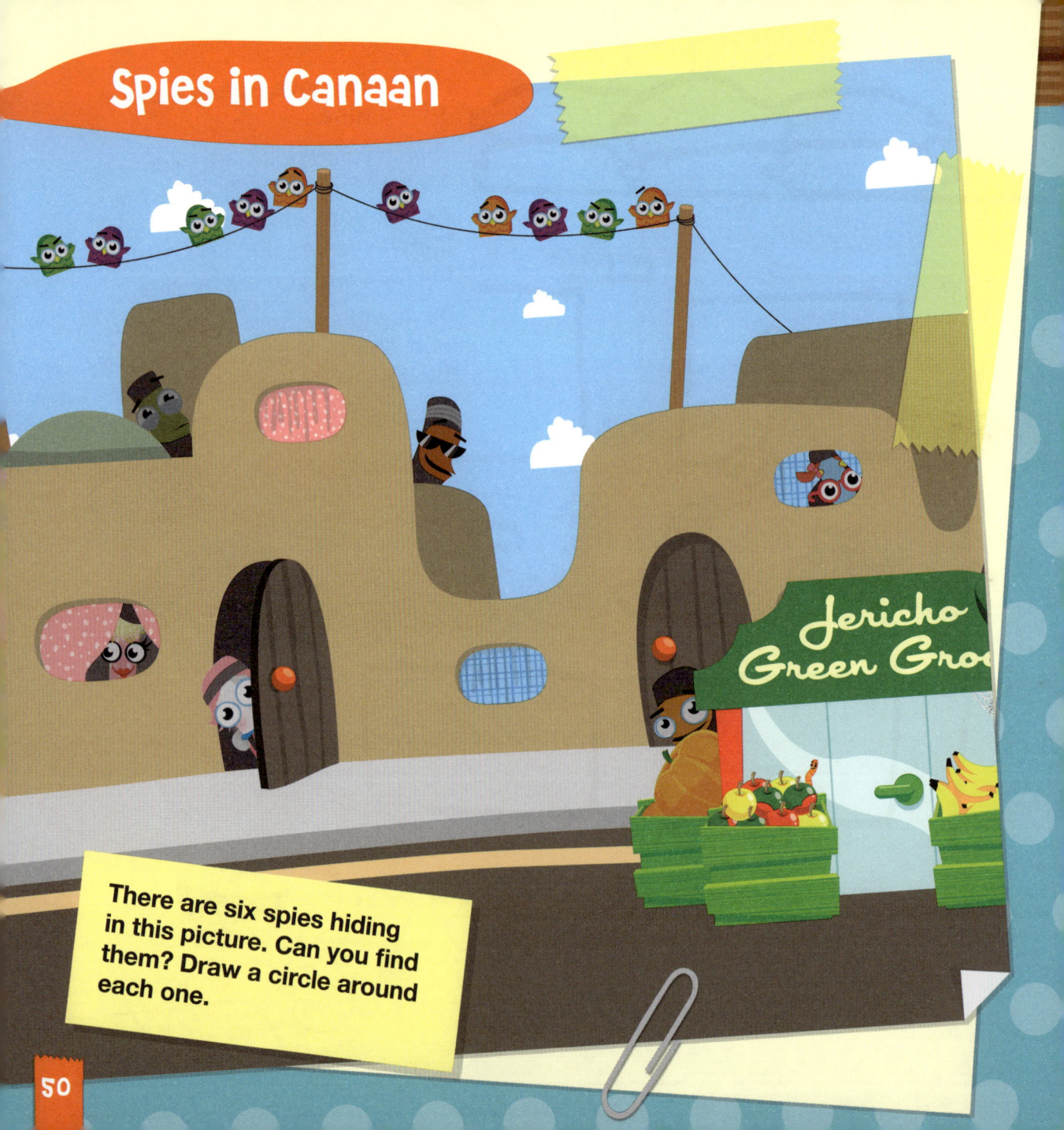

Spies in Canaan

Jericho Green Gro[cer]

There are six spies hiding in this picture. Can you find them? Draw a circle around each one.

50

Pens are playing hide-and-seek. Colour the shapes with dots in to see which Pen is hiding.

Gideon, the Brave and Mighty
Judges 6 and 7

God's friends, the Israelites, had some enemies. They were called Midianites because they came from a place called Midian. God needed someone to help His people escape from them.

But the man God chose was scared. His name was Gideon.

'I am with you, Gideon,' God said. 'You brave and mighty man! I want you to rescue my people.'

Gideon didn't feel brave or mighty. But he listened to God's plan. He chose to do as God said. And he was very surprised when 32,000 men came to help him!

God told Gideon to send some of them home.

So Gideon did – until only 300 men were left.

'How can I rescue Your people now?' Gideon asked.

'Just trust me,' answered God.

Gideon, the Brave and Mighty

That night, God said, 'Let's rescue my people!'

Gideon gave each of his men a trumpet and a pot with a flaming torch inside.

When Gideon blew his trumpet, his men blew theirs.

When Gideon threw his pot on the ground, his men threw theirs.

When Gideon waved his flaming torch in the air, his men waved theirs.

When Gideon yelled – so did his men.

The Midianites were terrified!

'What's all that noise?' shouted one.

'What's all that fire?' cried another.

'Who's doing all that shouting?' screamed yet another.

The Midianites were so afraid that they ran away. They thought a huge army was after them – not just 300 men!

God's plan had worked. He'd chosen the right man to rescue His people. And the right man had chosen to trust God: Gideon, the brave and mighty.

Gideon, the Brave and Mighty

Pens are using their lanterns to pretend to be Gideon's men. Colour in the picture and make the lanterns bright enough to scare away the Midianites.

Denzil isn't sure what a trumpet looks like. Can you help him? Put a tick beside the picture of the trumpet.

A Baby for Hannah
1 Samuel 1

Hannah wanted a baby. More than anything else in the world.

Every year, she and her husband went to a special place called Shiloh. Lots of people met there to pray and to worship God.

But one year at Shiloh, Hannah was so miserable she didn't even feel like eating.

'Everywhere there are children,' she sobbed. 'But I have none. I want a baby SO MUCH.'

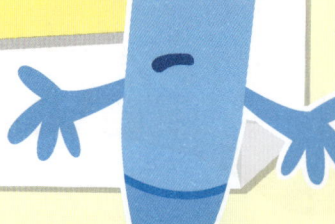

Hannah talked to God. And tears rolled down her cheeks.

'Lord, I'm *so* sad!' she cried. 'I want a baby. Please give me a son. If You do, I promise to bring him here to Shiloh when he is old enough. Then he can work for You.'

Eli, the priest, saw how unhappy Hannah was.

'I pray that God will give you what you've asked for,' he said.

A Baby for Hannah

When Hannah had finished talking to God, she felt better. She was sure He had listened to her. She knew He loved her, and she could trust Him to do what was best.

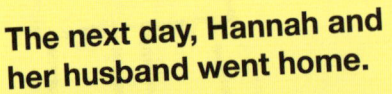

The next day, Hannah and her husband went home.

But they hadn't been back long when God answered Hannah's prayer! He gave her a son, and she called him Samuel.

Hannah loved Samuel.

But she loved God, too, and she'd made Him a promise.

'Samuel,' she said one day. 'Now you are old enough, I must take you to Shiloh to work for God there.'

Hannah was sad to leave Samuel, but she visited him every year.

And because she'd kept her promise to God, He gave her more children – brothers and sisters for her very first baby.

A Baby for Hannah

There are seven differences between these two pictures. Can you find them all? Draw a circle around each one.

Add up the numbers of baby toys.

3 + 1 =

2 + 3 =

4 + 2 =

3 + 3 =

5 + 3 =

A New King
1 Samuel 16

God had chosen a king for the country of Israel. His name was Saul.

But he wasn't a good king any more. He didn't listen to God.

So God decided to make someone else king of Israel instead.

God said to His friend, Samuel, 'Go to Bethlehem and find a man called Jesse. I've chosen one of his sons to be the new king.'

Samuel was afraid. What would Saul do if he found out that Samuel was going to look for a new king?

But Samuel trusted God. So he did as he was told.

When he arrived in Bethlehem, he found Jesse.

He met seven of Jesse's sons.

But none seemed to be the man God had chosen to be the new king.

A New King

'These aren't the men I'm looking for,' said Samuel to Jesse. 'Do you have any more sons?'

'Yes,' replied Jesse. 'My youngest is called David. He's looking after the sheep.'

'Ask him to come here,' said Samuel.

So David came in from the fields. He was strong and he looked healthy.

And God said to Samuel, 'This is the one! He will be the new king.'

Samuel nodded.

Then David's brothers watched as he poured some olive oil onto David's head. This was to show that David was the one God had chosen. One day, he would be the new king of Israel.

All at once, God's Holy Spirit came to live inside David.

And from that moment, David knew that God would be with him every single day.

A New King

Here are some of David's sheep.

How many sheep have long tails?

How many sheep have short tails?

How many sheep have no tails?

How many sheep have fluffy feet?

How many sheep have horns?

Some of the Pens are learning how to knit. But their wool has become tangled up. Can you help them work out whose ball of wool is whose? Write the number beside the right name.

Marco

Charlotte

Philippa

Max

Solomon, the Wise
1 Kings 2 and 3

David was king of Israel for forty years. He was a great ruler who loved God.

When David grew old, he made his son, Solomon, the new king.

'Solomon,' David said, 'you must listen to God and obey Him. Then He will be able to help you wherever you go, and with everything you do.'

So King Solomon did just as his father had told him to.

God was pleased with the new king. So pleased, that one night, He spoke to him in a dream.

'I want to give you a present,' God said. 'What would you like?'

Solomon could have asked for anything. But he thought very carefully before he answered.

'My father, David, was a great king,' Solomon said. 'He trusted You and You loved him.'

Solomon, the Wise

Then Solomon prayed, 'Now You have let me take over from him as king of Your special people, the Israelites. But I have no idea how to rule! So, please, God, I should like to have wisdom. If I am to be a great king like my father, I need to be wise.'

God listened to Solomon and He smiled.

'You will be the wisest man who has ever lived,' God said. 'And because you have been so unselfish, I will make you rich, too. You will be the most respected of all kings. And if you obey me, I will give you a long life.'

When Solomon woke from his dream, he knew God had spoken to him. So off he went to praise Him.

Solomon, the Wise

King Solomon is sitting on a very special seat called a 'throne'. Join the dots to see how grand it is!

Pens are having great fun pretending to be kings and queens. Help them look really royal by colouring in their crowns and robes.

Nehemiah Builds a New City
Nehemiah 1 and 2

Nehemiah was sad.

A long time ago, the city of Jerusalem had been destroyed in a war.

The walls all around it needed mending. The houses needed rebuilding. Then God's people could live there safely again.

Nehemiah wanted to go to Jerusalem to join in with the work.

So he prayed, 'Lord God, please help me so that I can help Your people.'

Nehemiah worked for the emperor, who was very fond of him.

One day, the emperor said, 'You look sad, Nehemiah. What's wrong?'

Nehemiah prayed, 'Lord God, please be with me while I talk to the emperor.'

Then, 'Your Majesty, may I go to Jerusalem?' he asked. 'The people there need my help to rebuild their city.'

The emperor looked thoughtful.

'Yes,' he nodded at last. 'You may go.'

Nehemiah Builds a New City

Nehemiah knew God was helping him, so he asked, 'Your Majesty, may I have some wood from your forests, too? If we have enough, we'll be able to finish all the work.'

'Yes, Nehemiah,' the emperor nodded again. 'And my soldiers will go with you to keep you safe on your journey.'

Late at night, Nehemiah rode around Jerusalem on a donkey. He looked at the broken walls and buildings.

Then he said to God's people, 'Let's rebuild the city! God has already helped me through the emperor's kindness. He won't leave us now!'

God's enemies sneered at their work.

But Nehemiah kept asking God for help.

And God stayed with them, until the rebuilding of Jerusalem was finished.

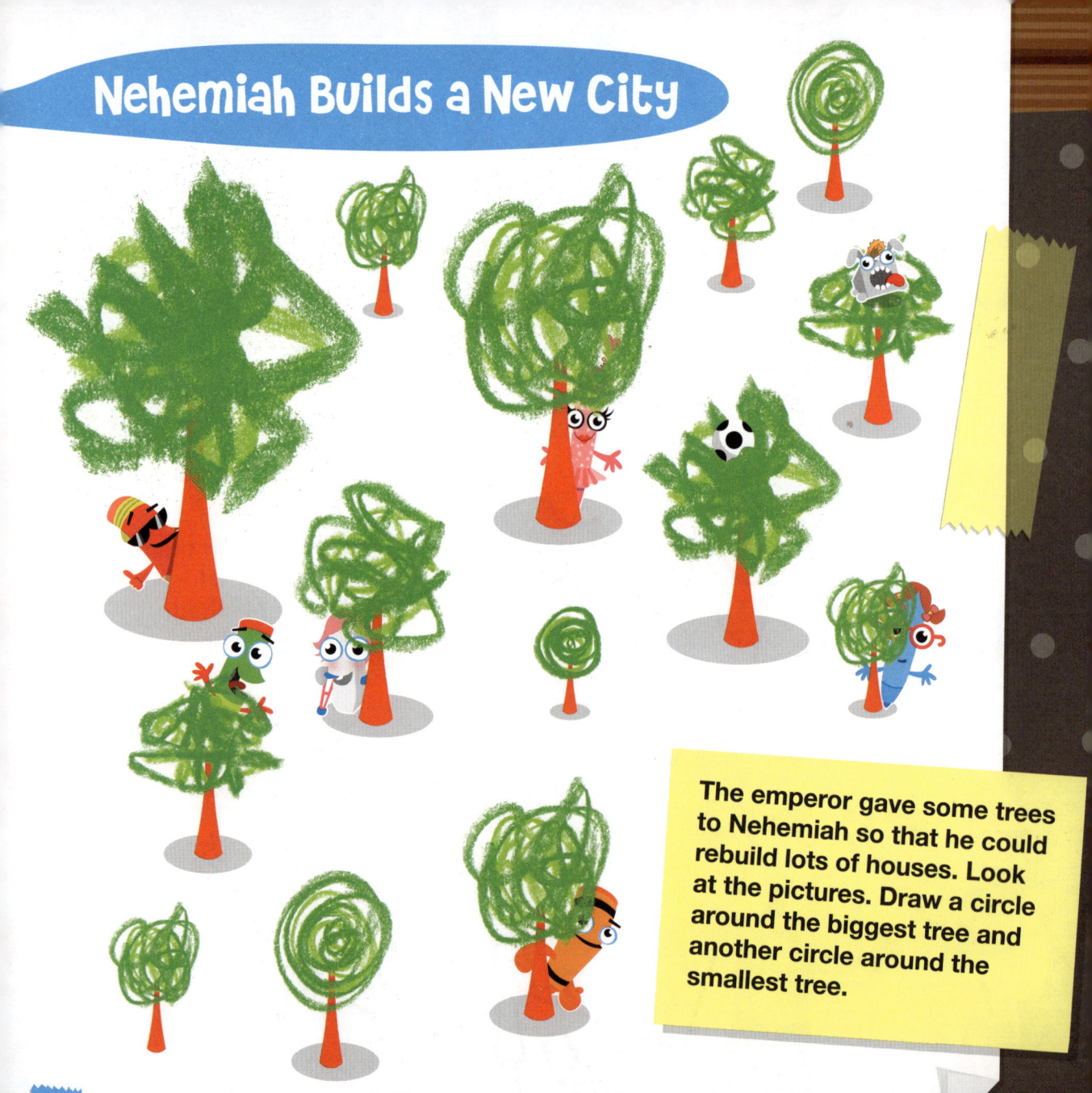

Nehemiah Builds a New City

The emperor gave some trees to Nehemiah so that he could rebuild lots of houses. Look at the pictures. Draw a circle around the biggest tree and another circle around the smallest tree.

80

Here is part of the city wall Nehemiah is helping to rebuild around Jerusalem. How many stones are missing? Put a tick next to the right answer.

- ⬭ Seven
- ⬭ Nine
- ⬭ Ten

The Man God Chose
Jeremiah 1 and 38

One day, God said to a man called Jeremiah: 'There are things I want you to tell my people.'

Jeremiah was worried.

'How can I do that, Lord?' he mumbled. '*I don't know what to say.*'

'Don't be afraid,' answered God. 'I will be with you. I will take care of you. And I will tell you what I want you to say.'

God was very sad.

He had been kind to His people. He had looked after them and He had helped them.

But they had stopped listening to Him. They didn't do as He asked them to. Or live the way He wanted them to.

Now God wanted Jeremiah to tell them to turn back to Him.

To be His friends again.

The Man God Chose

The people Jeremiah spoke to didn't like what he had to say.

They didn't want to hear God's message.

So they dropped poor Jeremiah down a well. It was deep and dark and cold. There was no water inside it, just mud. And Jeremiah sank down into it.

But God had told Jeremiah not to be afraid.

He'd told Jeremiah He would take care of him.

Before long, a servant at the palace went to see the king.

'Your Majesty, Jeremiah has been thrown into a well,' he said. 'It's not right. We can't leave him there.'

'Find three men to go with you,' ordered the king. 'Then help Jeremiah.'

With ropes, Jeremiah was pulled up out of the mud. Up out of the well.

God had chosen him.

God was with him.

The Man God Chose

Look at the well in the picture.

- How many orange bricks are there?
- How many red bricks are there?
- How many yellow bricks are there?

Join the dots to find out which Pens are having a rope-climbing race.

Who do you think will reach the top first? (Trace over the letters.)

Now colour in the picture.

87

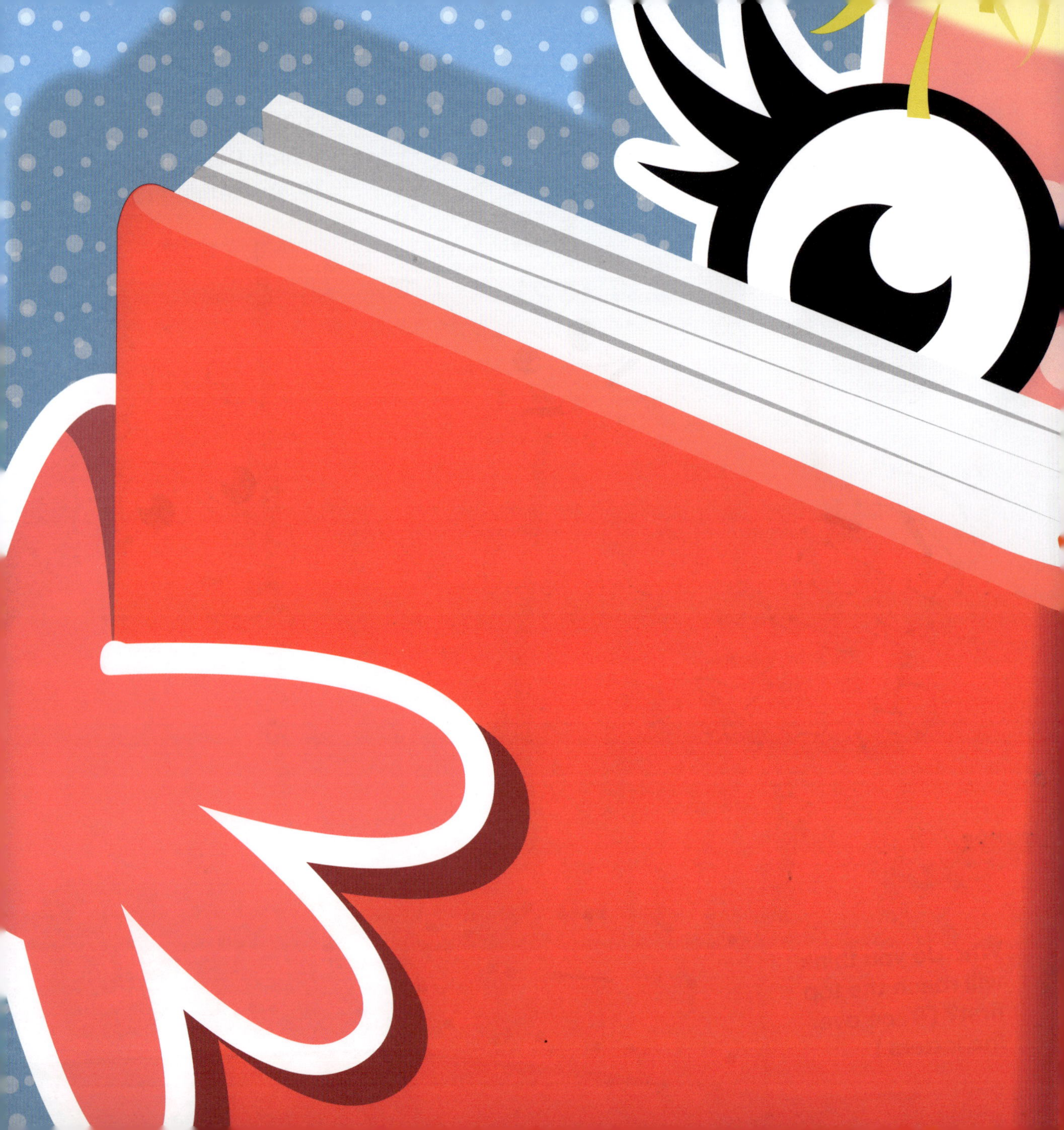

The New Testament

The Baby in the Stable
Matthew 1 and 2, Luke 1 and 2

'Hello, Mary!' cried an angel called Gabriel.

A young girl, called Mary, was very surprised!

'God is sending a new baby into the world,' Gabriel beamed. 'His very own Son. He will be King of the Earth. And God's chosen YOU to be His mother! You're to call Him, Jesus.'

An angel spoke to a man called Joseph, too.

'God wants you to marry Mary,' the angel said. 'Together you can look after God's Son.'

When it was nearly time for Jesus to be born, Mary and Joseph had to make a journey.

'The emperor wants to know how many people there are,' said Joseph. 'We must go to Bethlehem to be counted.'

But when they arrived, the town of Bethlehem was already packed with visitors. There was nowhere left to stay. So one kind innkeeper let them rest in his stable.

The Baby in the Stable

It was there, among the animals and the straw, that Jesus, the Son of God, was born.

Mary put Him gently down to sleep in the animals' feeding box.

That same night, some shepherds were looking after their sheep in the fields outside Bethlehem.

Suddenly, the skies lit up and another angel appeared!

'God's Son has been born!' the angel cried. 'He'll save people from the wrong things they do. He'll bring peace and happiness. And God's chosen *you* to be His first visitors!'

The shepherds hurried off excitedly to find Him.

Some wise men visited Jesus, too. A brand-new star in the sky led them to Him.

They gave Him presents of gold and frankincense and myrrh.

King Jesus really was very special.

The Baby in the Stable

Who is hiding in the stars? Start at star number one and join them all up to find out.

Marco is an angel in Pens' Christmas play. Here he is in his costume. Colour him in.

The Boy Who Wasn't Lost
Luke 2

Mary and Joseph were on a journey. A journey home to Nazareth.

There were lots of people with them. They'd all been to Jerusalem to a big festival called Passover. God's people joined in with the festival every year to celebrate His love for them.

Mary and Joseph had taken their young Son, Jesus.

But on their way home, they couldn't find Him.

'Is Jesus with you?' they asked some friends.

'No,' they answered. 'Sorry.'

'Well, where can He be?' Mary wondered. 'Someone *must* have seen Him.'

But no one had.

Jesus was missing.

'He's only twelve years old,' Mary worried. 'Whatever can have happened?'

'Let's go back to Jerusalem,' Joseph replied. 'Perhaps He's still there.'

The Boy Who Wasn't Lost

Back in the city, they searched for Jesus everywhere.

Suddenly – 'There He is!' Mary and Joseph cried.

Jesus was sitting on the floor in the Temple.

He was listening to the teachers talking about God. But He had lots to *say* about God, too.

Everyone was amazed. This young boy of twelve seemed to know so much.

'We've been looking for You, Jesus!' cried Mary. 'We were so worried.'

Jesus was surprised that His parents seemed upset.

'Why did you have to look for me?' He asked. 'The Temple is my Father's house. Where else would I be?'

As Jesus grew up back in Nazareth, He obeyed His parents. He learnt more and more about God, and everyone liked Him.

One day, He would be ready to teach people about His Father God.

The Boy Who Wasn't Lost

Pens Town

Jesus wasn't really lost, but Sticky is. He's on holiday and has been to the seaside. Only now he can't find his way back to Pens' town. Can you show him how to get there?

Mary and Joseph found Jesus in the Temple.

Help Marco find his bicycle by colouring the shapes with dots.

The First Followers
Luke 5

Crowds of people stood by the lake.

They wanted to see Jesus. They wanted to hear what He had to say about God.

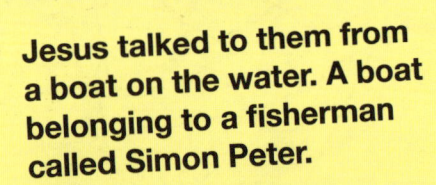

Jesus talked to them from a boat on the water. A boat belonging to a fisherman called Simon Peter.

When He'd finished teaching, Jesus said, 'Now, Simon Peter. Let's go fishing.'

Simon Peter glanced at his brother, Andrew, who was in the boat with them. He was a fisherman, too.

'No point,' Simon Peter grumbled. 'We fished all night and caught nothing.'

But Jesus wanted them to try again. So they sailed further out onto the lake and dropped their nets into the water.

'Waste of time,' Simon Peter thought. 'We won't catch anything.'

The First Followers

Suddenly –

'There's a fish!' Andrew hissed.

'There's another!' murmured Simon Peter.

And before they knew it, their nets were more full of fish than they'd ever thought possible!

They even had to call fishermen, James and John, over to help them pull in the catch!

On the beach again, Simon Peter knelt down in front of Jesus.

'You must be the Son of God,' he whispered. 'How else could we have caught so many fish? But why would You help *me*? I'm not a good man.'

Jesus smiled. 'People need to know how much God loves them,' He replied. 'We've caught fish together. Now let's go and catch people and help them make friends with Him!'

Jesus walked away. And the four fishermen followed Him.

The First Followers

Look carefully at these eight fish. Which is the odd one out? When you've found it, draw a circle around it.

106

Which Pens are looking at fish in the Pens' town Aquarium? Join the dots to find out.

Just Like Mary
Luke 10

One day, Jesus visited a village where two sisters called Martha and Mary lived.

When Martha saw Jesus coming, she hurried out to meet Him.

'Welcome to our village!' she beamed. 'Please come and have something to eat at our house. My sister, Mary, and I, would love You to spend some time with us.'

108

Mary was so excited when Jesus walked in! Straight away, she stopped doing the housework, took off her apron and washed her hands.

'Come and sit down, Lord,' she smiled.

Then she settled herself on the floor to listen to every word Jesus spoke. What a special visitor He was! Nothing was more important than spending time with Him.

Just Like Mary

Martha didn't sit down with Mary and listen to Jesus. There were lots of jobs to do – sweeping and dusting, washing and cooking.

When Martha saw that Mary had stopped working now that Jesus was there, she was cross.

'Why must I do everything?' she complained. 'I'm sure what You have to say is very interesting, Lord. But please ask Mary to come and help me.'

Jesus smiled at Martha. She looked hot and bothered.

'Martha,' He said kindly, 'thank you for inviting me into your home. But you must stop worrying about everything. And don't be cross with your sister,' He added. 'I know jobs need doing, but sometimes we can be too busy. Sometimes the best thing to do is simply to sit down and spend time with me. Just like Mary.'

Just Like Mary

Gloria has housework to do, just like Martha and Mary. Put a tick beside the things she *will* need to do her cleaning, and a cross beside the things she *won't* need.

Mary loves listening to Jesus! Colour in the picture.

God's Love
Matthew 6

Crowds of people wanted to hear Jesus talk about God. So He climbed a hill where they could see Him, and began to teach them.

'Do you want to be rich or do you want to be God's friends?' Jesus asked. 'Money and the things you buy won't last. Only ONE THING lasts forever: God's love. Let's try to live the way He wants us to.'

Then Jesus asked, 'Why do you worry that you won't have enough food to eat? Or that you won't have any clothes to wear? Do you think God doesn't care about you? It's time to *stop* worrying,' Jesus smiled. 'Do you see all the birds? They don't worry about what they're going to eat. God looks after them. So you can be sure that He'll look after you.'

God's Love

'Look at the wild flowers,' Jesus added. 'They're much more beautiful than a king's clothes! God dresses the flowers. Just think how much *more* He cares that YOU should be well-dressed, too!

'So now you know that you don't have to worry about anything,' Jesus beamed. 'Talk to God instead. Love God and do as He asks you to. Then He can give you everything you need.'

Jesus had lots more to say to the people who were listening to Him. There was so much He wanted to tell them about God.

'You don't need to worry about today,' He explained. 'And you don't need to worry about tomorrow either. God will be with you.'

God's Love

How many birds can you find in the picture?

a

b

c

d

Which flower has the most petals?

Now colour in all four flowers.

The Seed Story
Mark 4

'Let me tell you a story about a farmer,' Jesus said.

'As the farmer planted his seeds, some of them fell on the path around his field. They didn't grow there. The birds flew down and ate them.

'More seeds dropped among stones. Little green shoots sprang up. But there wasn't enough earth for them to grow proper roots. So when the sun shone, the shoots quickly dried up.

'Other seeds landed in weeds where there wasn't enough space or light. They couldn't grow properly.

'But some seeds,' said Jesus, 'fell where the earth was good and deep.

'Now, *their* shoots would grow up tall and strong.'

The people listening to Jesus looked puzzled.

'What does Your story mean?' they asked.

The Seed Story

Jesus replied, 'When some people hear about God, they are like the seeds that fell onto the path and were eaten by birds.

'They don't care. They don't want to listen. They won't make friends with Him.

'Other people are like the seeds dropped among stones. They are happy to hear about God at first. But they don't stay close to Him. They stop talking to Him.'

Jesus added, 'As for the seeds that landed in weeds, they are like people who hear about God, but never learn to trust Him.

'Some people, however,' Jesus smiled, 'listen to God and ask Him to be their Friend. They tell others about His love. They know they'll be with Him forever. They are like the seeds that fell onto good earth.

'The seeds that make God smile.'

The Seed Story

Look carefully at the picture. Can you find the twelve seeds hidden in it? Draw a circle around each one.

The seeds that were planted here have grown into pretty flowers.

Join the dots to see what each one looks like. Then colour them in.

The One Who Came Back
Luke 17

Jesus was walking to Jerusalem.

As He came to a village, He saw some men shuffling slowly towards Him.

Jesus counted them.

'Ten,' He thought.

When the ten men spotted Jesus, they stopped.

Straight away, Jesus realised why. They had a horrible skin disease that was very easy to catch. So they had to stay away from other people.

Suddenly, the men recognised Jesus.

'Please help us!' they cried. 'You can make us better.'

Jesus smiled. 'They have such faith in God,' He thought. And He spoke quietly to God about the sick men.

When He'd finished, He said to them, 'Go and find a priest who serves God in the Temple. Ask him to look at you. He'll be able to tell you if you're better.'

The One Who Came Back

The ten men glanced at each other. They didn't look different. They didn't *feel* different. But they did as Jesus told them to and went to find a priest.

The very next time the men looked at each other, they couldn't believe their eyes.

'You're better!' cried one.

'So are you!' beamed another.

'We ALL are!' laughed a third.

Their skin was smooth again. The disease had gone.

The ten men were *so* happy!

But only one of them rushed back to Jesus.

'Jesus!' he yelled. 'Look at me, I'm better! Thank You!'

'Where are the others?' Jesus asked. 'I healed ten of you. Why haven't the other nine come to say thank You, too?'

Then He added kindly, 'You are well again because you trusted me. I'm glad you came back to find me.'

The One Who Came Back

Pens are saying 'thank you' with giant letters. Help by colouring them in.

Sharpy has hidden ten of Gloria's hats. Can you find them? Draw a circle around each one.

The Water-Walker
Matthew 14

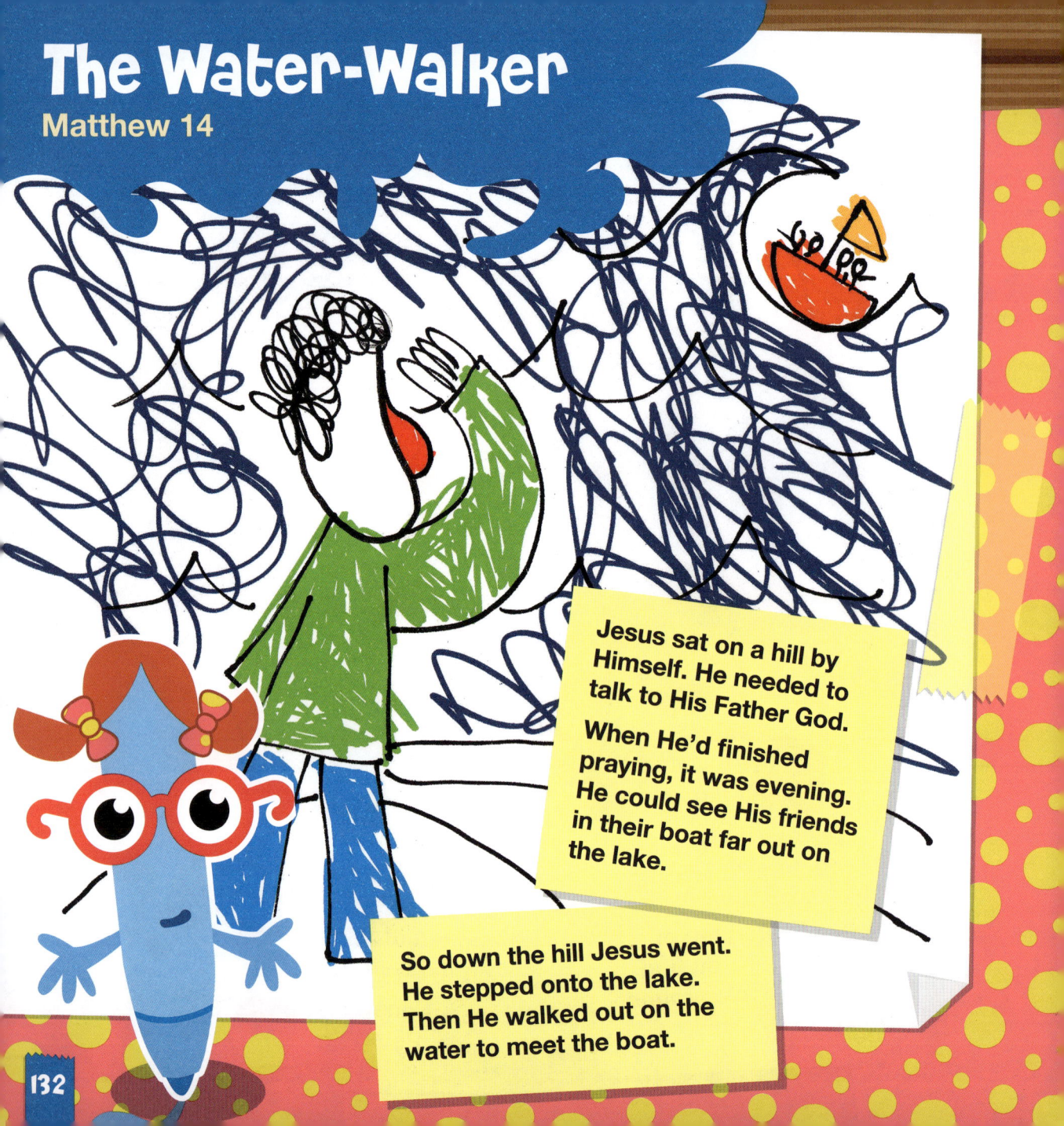

Jesus sat on a hill by Himself. He needed to talk to His Father God.

When He'd finished praying, it was evening. He could see His friends in their boat far out on the lake.

So down the hill Jesus went. He stepped onto the lake. Then He walked out on the water to meet the boat.

It was dark and stormy.

Suddenly, Jesus' friends saw something coming towards them on the water!

'It must be a ghost!' they screamed.

Jesus called, 'It's me! Don't be afraid!'

Jesus' friend, Peter, was in the boat.

'Is it really You, Lord?' he shouted. 'If it is, tell me to get out of the boat and walk on the water to meet You.'

Jesus answered, 'Come on then, Peter!'

The Water-Walker

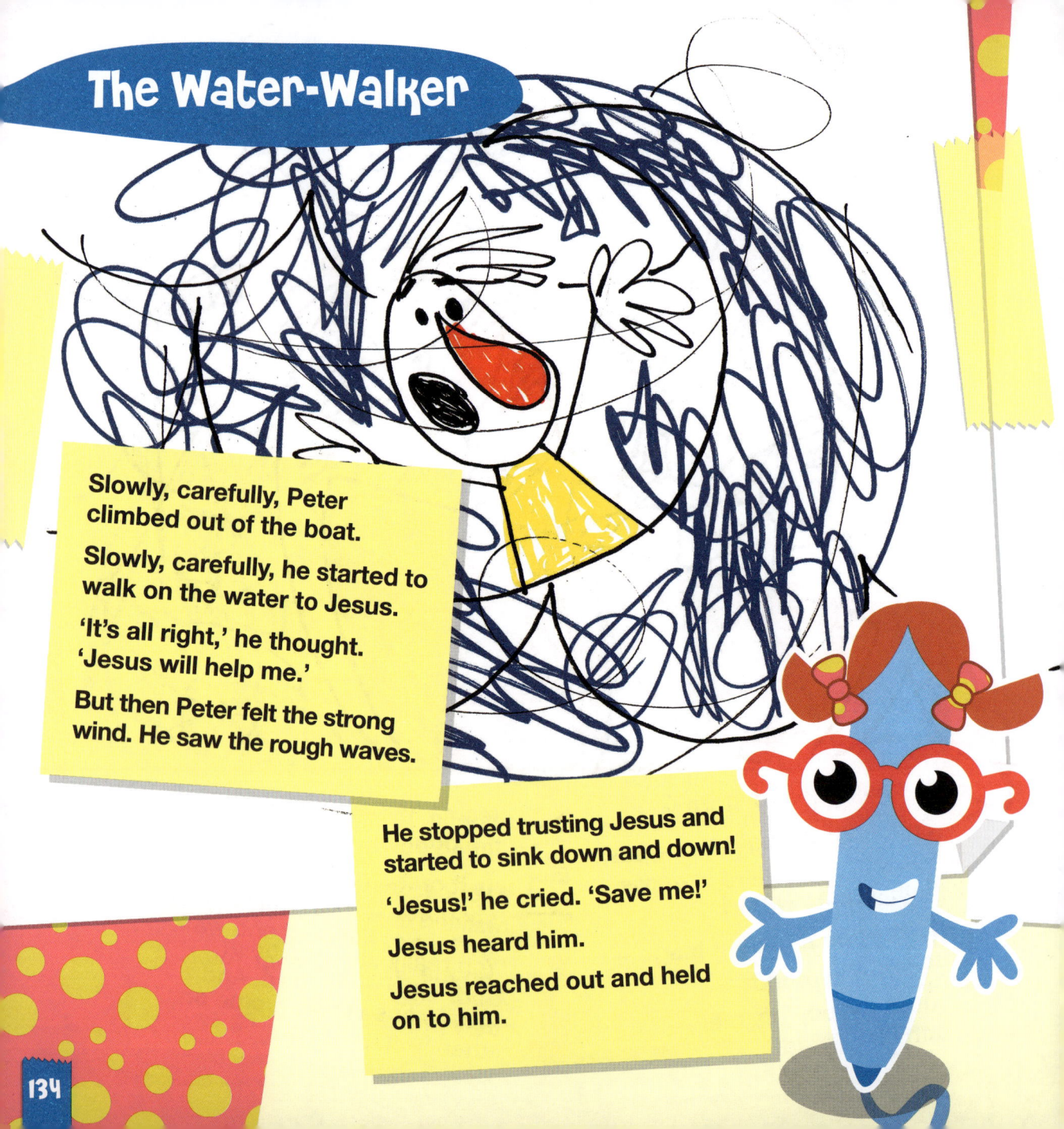

Slowly, carefully, Peter climbed out of the boat.

Slowly, carefully, he started to walk on the water to Jesus.

'It's all right,' he thought. 'Jesus will help me.'

But then Peter felt the strong wind. He saw the rough waves.

He stopped trusting Jesus and started to sink down and down!

'Jesus!' he cried. 'Save me!'

Jesus heard him.

Jesus reached out and held on to him.

'You don't trust me very much, do you, Peter?' Jesus smiled. 'Did you really think I would let you drown?'

He led Peter back to the boat and they climbed in.

At once, the stormy sea settled down.

At once, Jesus' friends realised how powerful He was.

'You really are the Son of God!' they murmured. And they praised Him.

The Water-Walker

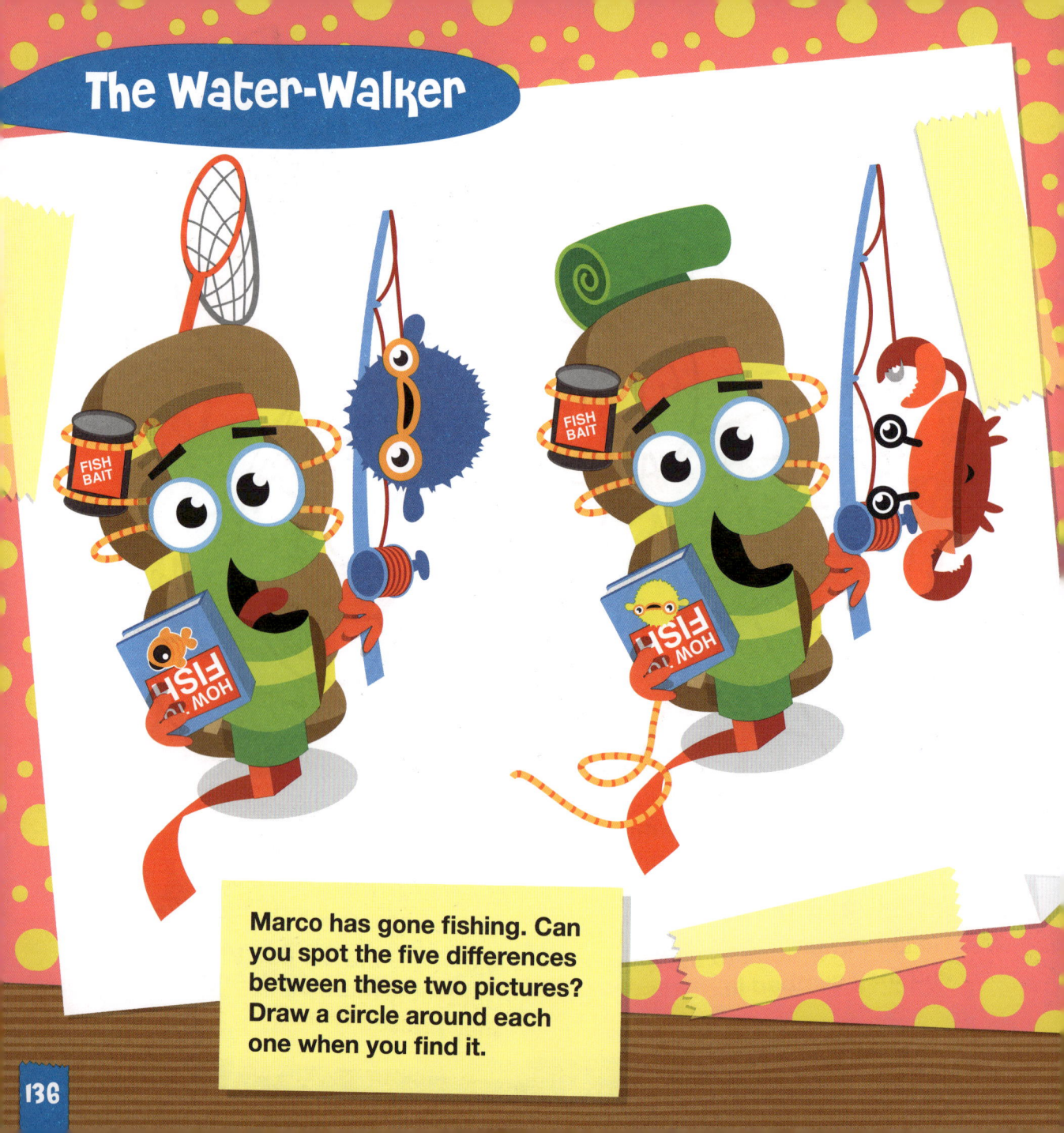

Marco has gone fishing. Can you spot the five differences between these two pictures? Draw a circle around each one when you find it.

Pens are on a river. What are they sitting in? Join the dots to find out!

Alive and Well!
John 11

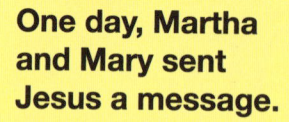

One day, Martha and Mary sent Jesus a message.

'Dear Jesus,' the message said, 'our brother, your good friend Lazarus, is very ill.'

Jesus loved Lazarus and his sisters, but He didn't seem worried.

Two days went by before He went with His disciples to visit them.

Jesus looked thoughtful. 'This has happened,' He said, 'to bring glory to God.'

When they arrived, Jesus knew that Lazarus had died.

'Jesus!' Martha cried. 'If only You'd been here, my brother would be alive! But even now, I know God will give You whatever You ask Him for.'

Mary knelt down at Jesus' feet and sobbed.

There were tears of sadness in Jesus' eyes, too.

Alive and Well!

People whispered, 'Jesus must have loved Lazarus very much.'

And they took Him to the cave where His friend was buried.

There was a rock in front of the opening.

'Move that stone out of the way,' Jesus said.

'Is that a good idea?' asked Martha. 'Lazarus has been buried for four days.'

Jesus said, 'You *will* see God's glory, Martha! Just believe that God has sent me!'

So the people watching rolled the rock away.

Jesus prayed, 'Thank You, Father, for listening to me. I want everyone here to hear me say this, so that they will believe You sent me.'

Then He called in a loud voice, 'Lazarus! Come out!'

Almost at once, Lazarus walked out of the cave!

Alive and well again.

Alive and Well!

Find the path Mary and Martha took to the cave where Lazarus was buried.

Jesus made Mary and Martha very happy when He brought Lazarus back to life. Colour the shapes with dots in to find out which Pen enjoys cheering up his friends, too.

The Fantastic Party
Luke 14

Jesus told a story about a man who held a huge party.

When everything was ready, the man said to one of his servants, 'Go and tell my guests it's party time!'

So off the servant went.

He found the invited guests. He smiled excitedly.

'The party's about to start!' he beamed.

But the guests shook their heads.

'I can't go,' muttered one. 'I've just bought a field. I must go and look at it.'

Another mumbled, 'And I've bought some oxen for my farm. I need to see them.'

'Sorry,' said a third man, 'but I've just got married.'

Every guest the servant asked said the same thing: 'Sorry.'

The Fantastic Party

Sadly, the servant told his master, 'No one's coming. They all have other things to do.'

The servant's master was cross.

'Then find people who *do* want to come,' he said. 'People who are poor or ill. Who can't walk or see. People no one cares about. Let's invite *them* to my party instead. I want my house to be full of those who *want* to be here.'

This time, all the people the servant invited said: 'Yes!'

Jesus told this story because He wanted everyone to know how much God loves them.

He wanted them to hear God's invitation: 'Come and be my friends today.'

He wanted everyone to answer: 'Yes, God.'

The Fantastic Party

Little Pens are having lots of fun at Hetty's birthday party. Can you guess what game they are playing?

Gloria has baked Hetty a birthday cake. Hetty is six years old today! Decorate the cake with your crayons so that it looks really yummy. Then draw six candles on the top.

149

Jesus in Jerusalem

Luke 19 and John 14

Jesus and His special friends were walking to the city of Jerusalem. They were going to celebrate an important festival. Lots of other people celebrated it, too. It was called Passover.

They were nearly there. But suddenly, Jesus stopped.

'There's a donkey tied up in the next village,' He said to His friends. 'I'd like two of you to fetch it for me. If anyone asks why you're taking it,' He added, 'just say that I need to borrow it for a while.'

When Jesus' friends brought the donkey to Him, Jesus climbed onto its back. Then He rode the rest of the way into Jerusalem.

Jesus in Jerusalem

There were people all along the road.

'Look!' they shouted excitedly. 'It's the Man God has sent to us! Praise Him!'

The crowds grew bigger and bigger. They threw their cloaks on the road for the donkey to walk on. They waved leaves from palm trees.

Everyone looked so happy to see Jesus.

But when it was time for the Passover festival, Jesus seemed sad.

'I must leave you soon,' He said to His friends.

'What do You mean?' asked Simon Peter. 'Where are You going?'

'Many people love me,' answered Jesus quietly. 'Many others hate me for what I teach about God. They will kill me. Afterwards, I'll go to be with my Father in heaven. But one day,' He smiled, 'you can be there, too.'

Jesus in Jerusalem

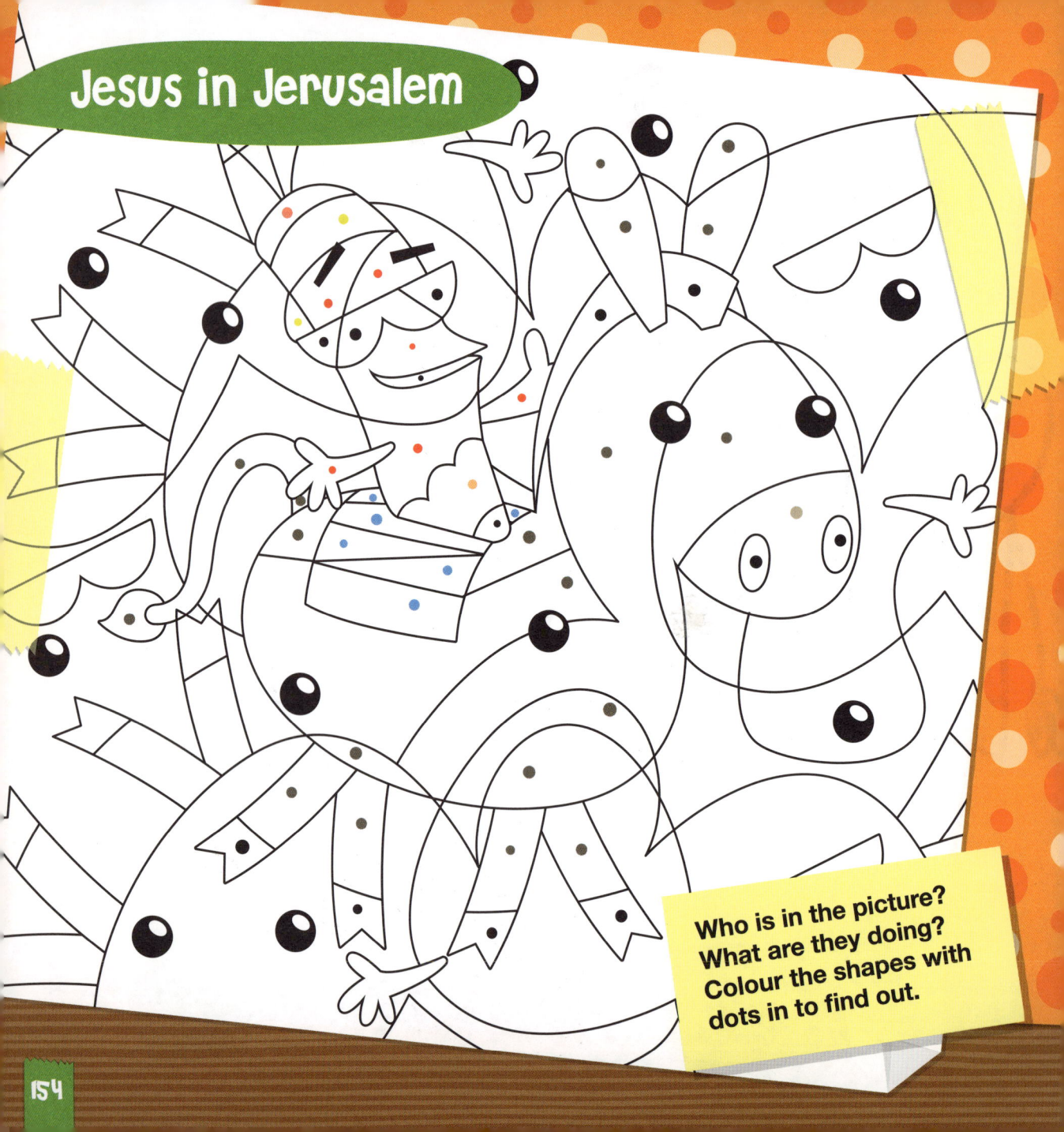

Who is in the picture? What are they doing? Colour the shapes with dots in to find out.

Help Jesus' two friends to find the donkey.

God's Great Plan
Mark 14 and 15, Luke 22, John 14

At the Passover festival, Jesus and His friends ate one last meal together.

Jesus shared out some bread.

'Eat this and remember me,' He said.

He passed round a cup of wine and added, 'Drink this and remember me, too.'

Then Jesus told His friends how much God loved them.

How much God loved everyone.

And He began to tell them why He had to die.

People couldn't be God's friends any more because they had done wrong things.

That's why God had made a plan. He would send His Son, Jesus, into the world to teach them all about Him.

And one day, Jesus would die to take away all those wrong things.

Then everyone could be God's friends again.

God's Great Plan

After their meal, Jesus and His friends walked to a garden. Jesus wanted to talk to God.

But suddenly a crowd of people with swords and clubs arrived. A man called Judas was with them.

Judas used to be one of Jesus' friends.

Not now.

'The Man I kiss is the one you want,' Judas told the crowd.

And he went to Jesus and kissed Him.

'Are You the Son of God?' a man asked Jesus – a man who hated Him.

'I am,' replied Jesus.

'No one can say that!' the man shouted. 'You're insulting God!'

Soldiers dragged Jesus away.

They hit Him. They made a crown out of thorny twigs and put it on His head.

They nailed Him to a wooden cross.

That's where Jesus died.

But God's plan wasn't finished …

God's Great Plan

Jesus and His friends are eating a meal. But there are five things wrong with the picture. Can you find them? Draw a circle around each one.

Pens are having a picnic. Who is eating what? Draw a line to match the right Pen with the right food.

Out of the Tomb!
Matthew 28

It was Sunday morning.

Three days after Jesus had died.

And it was early. Very early.

Two women went to see the tomb where Jesus was buried. They were both called Mary and they were Jesus' friends.

As they stood near the tomb, suddenly the ground started to shake. Then one of God's angels appeared!

A huge rock stood across the front of the tomb. The angel rolled it away.

'Look inside if you like,' the angel said, 'but Jesus isn't here. God has brought Him back to life – just as He planned.'

All at once, there Jesus was! He stood, smiling, right next to them.

'Don't be frightened,' Jesus said. 'Tell my friends to go to Galilee. That's where I'll meet them.'

Out of the Tomb!

The two women called Mary hurried away. And when Jesus' friends heard their news, off they went to Galilee.

There Jesus met them, just as He'd said He would.

When they saw Him, they couldn't believe their own eyes.

'It's true!' they cried. 'You're alive again!'

'Listen,' Jesus said. 'I've got a very important job for you to do.'

Jesus' friends gazed at Him.

'I want you to tell people everywhere all about me,' Jesus said. 'Teach them everything I've taught you. The whole world needs to know how much God loves them.

'Now, soon,' He added, 'it will be time for me to go to my Father in heaven. But you won't be on your own. Whenever you need me, I promise I'll be with you. Always.'

Out of the Tomb!

Jesus is alive! Colour in the picture.

The stone in front of the entrance to Jesus' tomb was VERY big and VERY heavy.

Look at these stones.

Which stone is the biggest? Put a tick beside it.

Which stone is the smallest? Put a cross beside it.

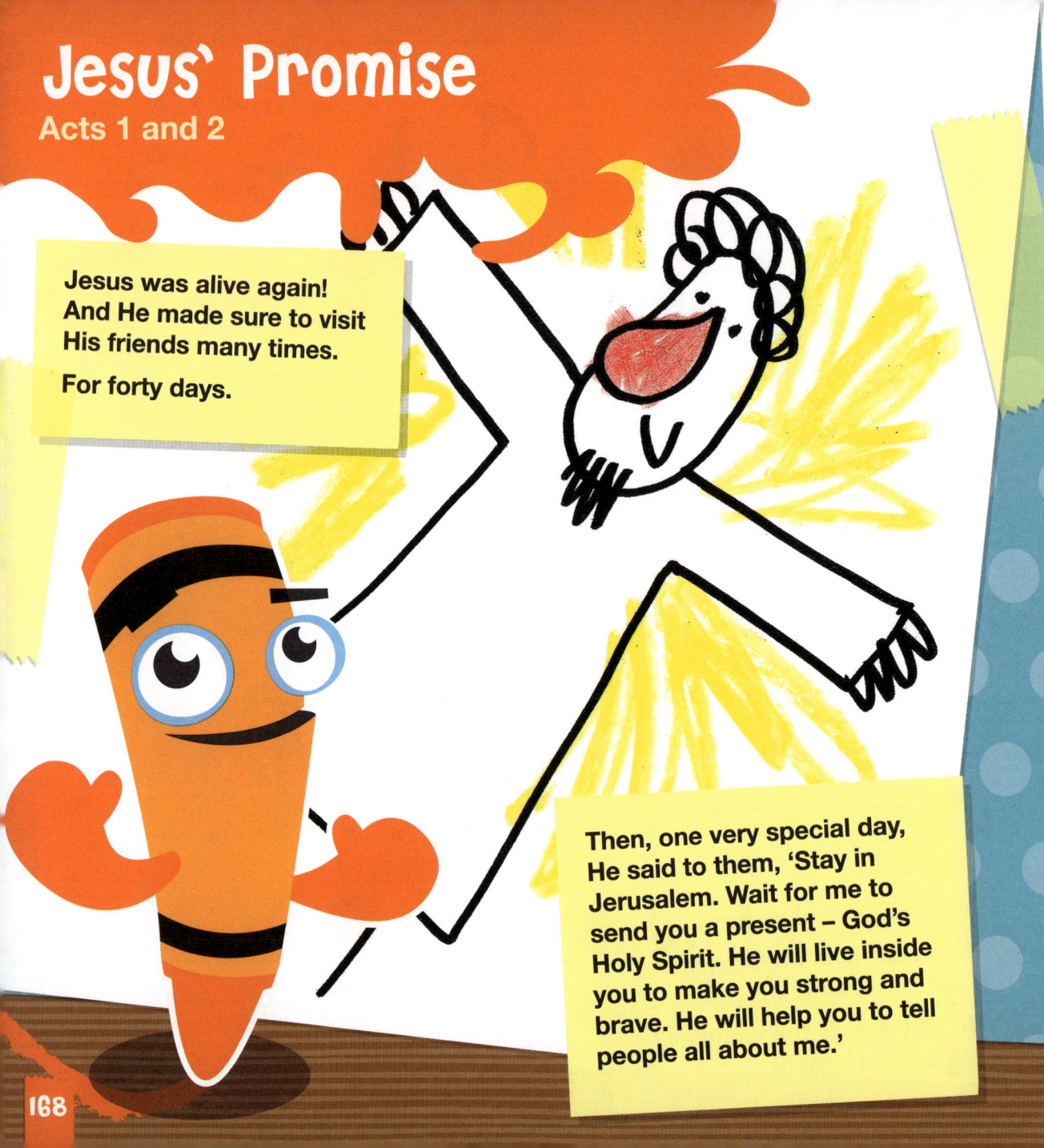

Jesus' Promise
Acts 1 and 2

Jesus was alive again! And He made sure to visit His friends many times.

For forty days.

Then, one very special day, He said to them, 'Stay in Jerusalem. Wait for me to send you a present – God's Holy Spirit. He will live inside you to make you strong and brave. He will help you to tell people all about me.'

Jesus finished speaking. And right there and then, God sent a cloud to lift Him up into heaven.

Jesus' friends didn't move. They just stared after Him.

Then two men dressed all in white came and stood next to them.

'Why are you looking into the sky?' they asked. 'Jesus has gone to be with His Father.'

Jesus' Promise

The men smiled.

'But He will come back!' they said. 'In just the same way as you've seen Him go.'

Jesus' friends did as He had told them to. He had promised that He would send God's Holy Spirit to them. So back they went to Jerusalem.

There they stayed.

There they waited.

As they sat together one day, they heard a noise. It sounded like a rushing wind. Flames of fire danced in the air. They touched everyone in the room.

Here He was! God's Holy Spirit!

Just as Jesus had said, He had come to live inside them.

To be their Helper.

To make them strong and brave.

To remind them that God would never let them go!

Jesus' Promise

Jesus has gone to be with His Father in heaven.

☐ How many orange birds can you see in the sky?

☐ How many green birds can you see?

☐ And how many clouds can you see?

What's that flying through the sky? Join the dots to see!

★ Old Testament Activity Answers ★

The Very Beginning Page 14

★ There are 11 sea creatures in the picture.

★ The crab has 10 arms and legs.

In God's Garden Pages 20-21

★ The odd snake out has a circle around it.

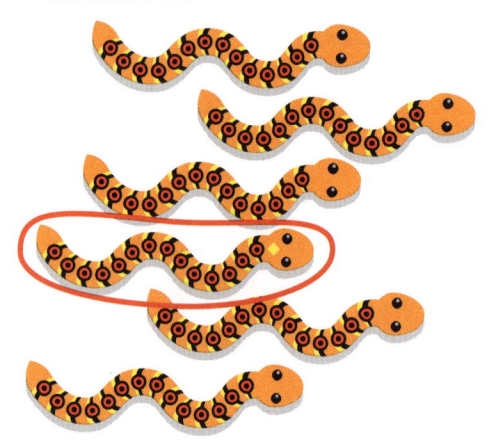

★ Charlotte is holding a banana.

When the Rain Came Down 26-27

★ Denzil is riding on a camel.

God's Good Friends Page 32

★ Gloria has 8 suitcases.

★ The biggest suitcase has a circle around it and the smallest suitcase has a square around it.

The Wrong Son Page 38

★ The odd one out has a tick beside it.

Moses, God's Hero Pages 44-45

★ Moses has: 7 sheep, 5 goats, and 12 animals altogether.

★ The 2 bushes that are the same are joined with a line.

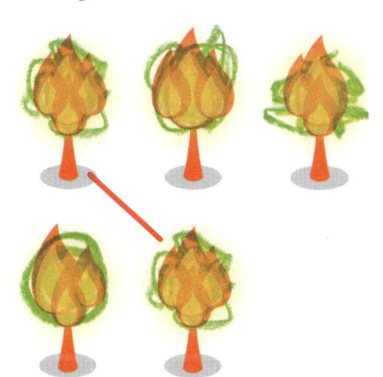

Spies in Canaan Pages 50-51

★ The 6 spies have circles around them.

★ Philippa Feltpen is hiding under the table.

Gideon, the Brave and Mighty Page 57

★ There is a tick beside the trumpet.

A Baby for Hannah Pages 62-63

★ The 7 differences have circles around them.

★ Answers to baby toy sums:
3 + 1 = 4
2 + 3 = 5
4 + 2 = 6
3 + 3 = 6
5 + 3 = 8

A New King Pages 68-69

★ 2 sheep have long tails.
4 sheep have short tails.
3 sheep have no tails.
1 sheep has fluffy feet.
5 sheep have horns.

★ Marco – 3
Charlotte – 2
Philippa – 4
Max – 1

Nehemiah Builds a New City Pages 80-81

★ The biggest and smallest trees have circles around them.

★ There are 9 stones missing.

The Man God Chose Pages 86-87

★ There are: 6 red bricks, 8 orange bricks, and 11 yellow bricks.

★ Denzil, Marco and Philippa are having a rope-climbing race. Marco will reach the top first.

★ New Testament Activity Answers ★

The Baby in the Stable Page 94
★ An angel is hiding in the stars.

The Boy Who Wasn't Lost Page 100

The First Followers Pages 106-107
★ The odd fish out has a circle around it.

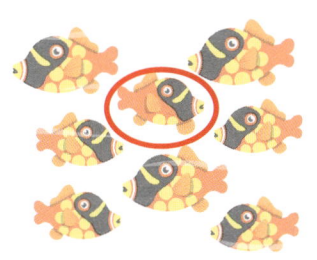

★ Max, Sharpy and Denzil are looking at fish.

Just Like Mary Page 112
★ The things Gloria will need have a tick beside them, and the things she won't need have a cross beside them.

God's Love Pages 118-119
★ There are 10 birds in the picture.
★ Flower b has the most petals.

The Seed Story Page 124

★ There are circles around the 12 seeds.

The One Who Came Back Page 131

★ There are circles around the 10 hats.

The Water-Walker Pages 136–137

★ The 5 differences have a circle around them.

★ Pens are sitting in a canoe.

Alive and Well! Pages 142–143

★

★ Marco enjoys cheering up his friends.

The Fantastic Party Page 148

★ Little Pens are playing pass-the-parcel.

Jesus in Jerusalem Pages 154–155

★ Denzil is riding on a donkey.

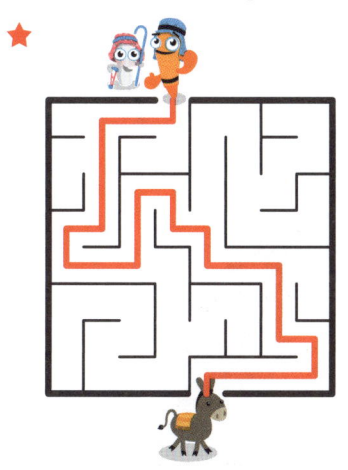

★

God's Great Plan Pages 160–161

★ The 5 wrongs things have a circle around them.

Lines join the right Pens to the right food.

Out of the Tomb! Page 167

★ There is a tick beside the biggest stone and a cross beside the smallest.

Jesus' Promise Pages 172–173

★ There are: 7 orange birds, 5 green birds, and 4 clouds.

★ A hot air balloon is flying through the sky.

179

www.meetpens.co.uk

Today in Pens' town

- How many birds on the telephone wire?
- What colour is Charlotte's flag?
- What is Sharpy chewing?
- Where is Max's football?

Join the Pens gang for lots of games and fun things to do.

www.meetpens.co.uk

You'll also find lots of other Pens books, devotions and a DVD to enjoy!